Mastering Trendline Strategies

A Forex Trader's Guide to Breakouts, Reversals, and Market Precision

By

Nathaniel J. Brooks

DISCLAIMER

This book is only designed for educational and informational purposes. It is intended to illustrate trading ideas, systems, and market insights gained through study and practice. It is not designed to provide personalised financial guidance or suggestions.

This book does not provide any financial, investing, legal, or trading advice. All techniques, charts, examples, and scenarios are offered solely for educational illustration and should not be regarded as recommendations to buy, sell, or hold any financial asset.

Trading in the foreign exchange market and other financial instruments entails risk, including the loss of funds. No method, strategy, or example presented in this book can guarantee success. Market conditions vary, and previous performance is no guarantee of future results or illustrations.

Readers are solely responsible for their trading decisions, risk management, and outcomes. Trading should only be done with funds that you can afford to lose. Readers are encouraged to seek financial expert guidance as needed.

All chart drawings in this book are based on publicly available market price data and are intended solely as analytical examples for educational purposes. Charts, tools, platforms, brokers, and software are only mentioned for instructional purposes. The author is not

Table of Contents

INTRODUCTION

The forex market never sleeps. Neither did I during my first year of trading. Back in 2009, I was staring at charts until 3 AM, desperate to find the secret formula that would unlock consistent profits. My account balance told a different story than my confidence. Down 40% in six months, I was ready to quit. Then something changed everything - a single diagonal line on my EUR/USD chart. That line wasn't fancy. It connected just three points over two weeks. But when price approached it for the fourth time, something magical happened. The market respected that line like an invisible barrier. Price bounced off it with such precision that I couldn't believe what I was seeing.

That was my first real encounter with trend lines. Not the textbook version, but the raw, profitable reality of how these simple tools can transform your trading. You might think trend lines are too basic. Too simple for the complexity of modern forex markets. I thought the same thing. After all, we live in an age of artificial intelligence, complex algorithms, and sophisticated trading systems. How could a simple line compete with all that technology? Here's what fifteen years of trading has taught me: the most powerful tools are often the simplest ones.

Why Trend Lines Still Matter

The forex market processes over $7 trillion in daily volume. Institutional traders, hedge funds, and central banks all participate in this massive ecosystem. Yet despite all the complexity, price still moves in predictable patterns. It still respects levels that thousands of traders are watching. Trend lines work because they represent collective human behavior. When you draw a line connecting significant highs or lows, you're mapping the psychology of every trader who bought or sold at those levels. You're identifying where pain and pleasure intersect in the market.

I remember trading the GBP/USD during the Brexit referendum period. Chaos everywhere. News headlines changing by the hour. Technical indicators spinning wildly. But there was one ascending trend line that had held for three weeks. Every time price approached it, buyers stepped in. That line became my anchor in the storm. The fourth time price tested that line, I loaded up on long positions. The bounce gave me 180 pips in two days. While other traders were paralyzed by uncertainty, I was following a simple line that told me exactly where institutional money was likely to defend.

What You'll Learn in This Book

This isn't another collection of theoretical concepts. Every strategy in this book has been tested with real money in real market conditions. Some cost me dearly. Others changed my life. You'll discover how to identify the trend lines that matter and ignore the ones that don't. There's a difference between drawing lines and drawing profitable lines. Most traders never learn this distinction. We'll explore breakout strategies that can capture explosive moves when trend lines finally give way. I'll share the exact criteria I use to separate genuine breakouts from false signals. The difference is worth thousands of pips over time.

Bounce trading will become your bread and butter. These setups offer excellent risk-reward ratios and happen frequently enough to provide consistent opportunities. You'll learn to spot the subtle signs that indicate when a trend line is about to hold versus when it's about to break. But technical skills alone won't make you profitable. We'll dive deep into the psychology of trend line trading. The patience required. The discipline needed. The mental frameworks that separate consistent winners from perpetual strugglers. Risk management gets its own detailed treatment because it's where most traders fail. You can have the best trend line system in the world, but without proper risk controls, you'll eventually blow up your account. I know because I've been there.

My Promise to You

I won't sugarcoat anything in this book. Trading is hard. Trend lines aren't magic wands that eliminate losses. They're tools that, when used correctly, can give you a significant edge in the markets. Some of the stories I'll share are painful. Like the time I ignored a clear trend line break and held onto a losing position for three weeks. Or when I risked too much on what seemed like a perfect setup and lost $15,000 in a single trade.

But there are victories too. The month I made 47% returns trading nothing but trend line bounces. The day I caught a 400-pip breakout on the AUD/JPY that paid for my daughter's college tuition. These experiences shaped my approach to trend line trading. They taught me that consistency matters more than home runs. That patience is more valuable than speed. That risk management is more important than profit maximization.

How to Use This Book

Each chapter builds upon the previous one. Start from the beginning even if you think you know trend lines. My approach might be different from what you've learned before. Practice every concept with small position sizes before risking significant capital. The market will always be there tomorrow. Your trading account might not be if you rush the learning process. Take notes. Keep a trading journal. Review your trades regularly. The combination of this book's strategies and your own disciplined practice will create a powerful foundation for long-term success. The forex market is waiting. Your trend lines are ready to be drawn. Let's begin this journey together.

CHAPTER 1

The Foundation - What Makes Trend Lines Work in Forex

The forex market operates on human psychology, and trend lines are the visual representation of that psychology. When you understand why these simple diagonal lines have power over trillion-dollar market movements, you'll start seeing opportunities that most traders miss completely.

The Psychology Behind Every Line

Every trend line tells a story of buyers and sellers fighting for control. When price touches a trend line and bounces, it's not magic - it's thousands of traders making the same decision at the same level. These traders remember previous prices. They know where they bought before. They know where they sold before. Most importantly, they know where they lost money before.

I've watched institutional traders place massive orders right at trend line levels. They're not guessing. They're following the same psychological principles that drive retail traders, just with bigger positions and better discipline. The difference is they trust what the line tells them instead of fighting against it.

You'll notice that strong trend lines often coincide with round numbers or previous support and resistance levels. This isn't coincidence. It's confluence - multiple reasons for the market to react at the same price level. The more reasons you have for a trend line to hold, the more likely it is to produce a profitable trading opportunity.

How Markets Create Trend Lines

Markets don't move in straight lines. They create swings - highs and lows that form the foundation of every trend line you'll ever draw. These swings happen because of the constant battle between bulls and bears. When bulls get exhausted, bears take control and push price lower. When bears run out of steam, bulls step in and drive price higher.

The most powerful trend lines connect at least three significant swing points. Two points create a line, but three points create a pattern. When you see price respect a trend line for the third time, you're witnessing the market's acceptance of that level as important. The fourth touch often provides the best trading opportunities because confidence in the line is highest.

Institutional Money and Trend Lines

Large institutional traders use trend lines differently than retail traders. They don't just look for bounces and breakouts. They use trend lines to determine where to accumulate or distribute large positions without moving the market against themselves. When you see a trend line holding multiple times, there's often institutional money defending that level.

Banks and hedge funds have teams of analysts drawing the same trend lines you're learning to draw. The difference is they have the capital to make those lines self-fulfilling prophecies. If enough institutional money believes a trend line will hold, they'll place orders that make it hold. If they believe it will break, they'll place orders that make it break.

This is why some trend lines seem to work better than others. The ones that work consistently are the ones that institutional money is watching and respecting. Your job is to identify these high-probability lines and trade alongside the smart money instead of against it.

Time Frames and Trend Line Strength

The time frame you use to draw trend lines directly affects their reliability. A trend line drawn on a monthly chart carries much more weight than one drawn on a 5-minute chart. This is because longer time frames represent more market participants and more trading decisions.

Daily charts offer the best balance between reliability and trading opportunities for most traders. They filter out much of the noise that makes shorter time frames unreliable, while still providing enough setups to keep you active in the markets. Weekly charts are excellent for identifying major trend lines that can guide your overall market bias.

However, you shouldn't ignore shorter time frames completely. Once you identify a strong trend line on the daily chart, you can use the 4-hour or 1-hour charts to fine-tune your entry and exit points. This multi-timeframe approach significantly improves your risk-reward ratios.

Setting Up Your Platform

Your trading platform setup can make or break your trend line analysis. You need clean charts that highlight price action without unnecessary clutter. Remove indicators that don't directly support your trend line decisions. Keep only the essential tools that help you identify and validate trend line setups.

Color coordination matters more than you might think. Use contrasting colors for your trend lines so they stand out clearly against your chart background. I use bright yellow for ascending trend lines and bright red for descending ones. This visual distinction helps me quickly assess market structure across multiple currency pairs.

The Market's Memory

The forex market has an excellent memory for significant price levels. A trend line that held six months ago might become relevant again when price returns to that area.

This is why you should never delete old trend lines from your charts. They might not be actively influencing current price action, but they could become critical support or resistance levels in the future.

Price often returns to test old trend lines after breaking through them. These retests provide some of the highest-probability trading setups you'll ever find. The market is essentially asking: "Is this level still important?" How price reacts to these retests tells you everything you need to know about the strength of the underlying trend.

Understanding these foundational concepts separates profitable trend line traders from those who struggle with consistency. You're not just drawing lines on a chart - you're mapping the collective psychology of market participants and positioning yourself to profit from their predictable behavior patterns.

CHAPTER 2

Drawing Your First Trend Line - The Art Behind the Science

Most traders draw trend lines wrong from day one. They connect any two points that seem significant and expect the market to respect their analysis. The reality is much different - the forex market only honors trend lines that align with genuine market structure and institutional money flow patterns.

Understanding Market Structure First

Before you draw a single trend line, you must understand how the forex market creates meaningful price swings. Every currency pair moves in waves - periods of buying pressure followed by selling pressure, creating the highs and lows that form your connection points. Not every high and low matters. Only swing points that represent actual shifts in market sentiment deserve your attention. A valid swing high occurs when price reaches a peak that's higher than at least two candles on each side. A valid swing low forms when price hits a bottom that's lower than at least two candles surrounding it. These formations show you where large participants changed their positions rather than where algorithmic noise created temporary movements.

My breakthrough with trend line accuracy came during year three of trading when I stopped chasing every small fluctuation. Instead, I learned to wait for clear structural breaks - moments when the market definitively changed direction with conviction. This patience eliminated most of my false signals and dramatically improved my risk-reward ratios on trend line trades.

Connection Methods That Actually Work

Once you've identified legitimate swing points, connecting them becomes a precise science. Ascending trend lines require linking successive higher lows that demonstrate increasing buyer interest. Each low point must be higher than the previous one, showing that demand strengthens as price rises. Descending trend lines connect successive lower highs that prove seller dominance is growing while buyer enthusiasm fades.

The slope of your trend line reveals critical information about the underlying trend's health. Extremely steep angles suggest unsustainable momentum that will likely fail quickly. Very shallow angles might be technically accurate but won't provide compelling trading opportunities because the risk-reward ratios become unfavorable. You need the slope that best captures the natural rhythm of institutional money movement in that particular market environment.

Chart 1: GBP/USD daily timeframe showing methodical trend line construction across three significant swing lows.

Chart 1 Reference Point: *The chart demonstrates proper angle selection, highlighting how each successive low maintains higher positioning than the previous touch point.*

Timeframe Selection Strategy

Your timeframe choice determines both the reliability and trading frequency of your trend line analysis. Daily charts provide the foundation for most successful trend line strategies because they filter out intraday noise while maintaining enough granularity for regular trading opportunities. This timeframe captures institutional decision-making cycles without getting caught up in algorithmic trading fluctuations that dominate shorter periods.

Weekly charts produce incredibly robust trend lines that can guide your market bias for months at a time. These longer-term lines often coincide with major psychological levels and round numbers that institutional money managers use for their large position entries and exits. However, weekly analysis generates fewer actionable setups throughout the year, requiring more patience than most active traders possess.

I've found that combining daily trend line identification with hourly chart timing creates the optimal balance between reliability and opportunity frequency. The daily chart shows you where institutional money is likely to act, while the hourly chart helps you time your entries with precision to maximize risk-reward ratios.

The Three-Touch Validation Process

A trend line becomes truly reliable only after surviving multiple tests from live market conditions. Your initial two touches create the basic line structure. The third successful test validates that other market participants recognize this level as significant. The fourth touch often provides your highest-probability trading setup because collective confidence in the line reaches maximum levels.

During my fifth trading year, I tracked over 200 trend line setups and discovered that lines with three or more successful tests produced winning trades 73% of the time. Lines with only two touches had a success rate below 45%.

This data convinced me to wait for proper validation before risking significant capital on any trend line trade.

Chart 2: Trendline Trade setup at the third successful test

Critical Construction Errors

The most destructive mistake traders make is continuously adjusting their trend lines after drawing them. Once you've identified a valid line based on proper structural analysis, moving it destroys its predictive value and turns objective analysis into subjective interpretation.

The market doesn't accommodate your convenience - it only respects levels that genuinely matter to institutional participants.

Another expensive error involves drawing lines that confirm your existing directional bias rather than reflecting actual price structure. Bullish traders unconsciously draw ascending lines that support long positions. Bearish traders find descending lines that justify short positions. This confirmation bias leads to poor trade selection and consistent losses over time.

The most profitable trend lines are the obvious ones that experienced traders can identify independently. These lines carry institutional weight because multiple large participants are monitoring the same structural levels. Focus on quality over quantity - a few well-constructed trend lines will serve you better than dozens of questionable connections.

CHAPTER 3

Support and Resistance - Where Price Respects Your Lines

Support and resistance through trend lines creates some of the most reliable trading opportunities in the forex market. These aren't mystical concepts - they represent real psychological levels where thousands of traders make buying and selling decisions simultaneously. Understanding why prices bounce off trend lines gives you a massive edge over traders who treat these levels as random events.

The Psychology Behind Price Respect

When price approaches a trend line that has held multiple times, something powerful happens in the collective trader mindset. Bulls who bought at previous bounces are watching to see if their strategy will work again. Bears who sold at previous rejections are preparing to add to their positions if the line holds. New traders are studying the same charts you're looking at, making similar decisions based on the same visual evidence. This creates self-fulfilling prophecies where trend lines work precisely because so many people believe they will work.

I learned this lesson during a particularly volatile period in 2016 when the GBP/USD was testing a major ascending trend line that had held for six weeks. Each time price approached this line, volume increased dramatically as traders positioned themselves for either a bounce or a break. The fourth test produced a 240-pip bounce in eighteen hours because institutional money was defending the level aggressively. That experience taught me that trend lines with multiple successful tests become increasingly powerful as more traders recognize their significance.

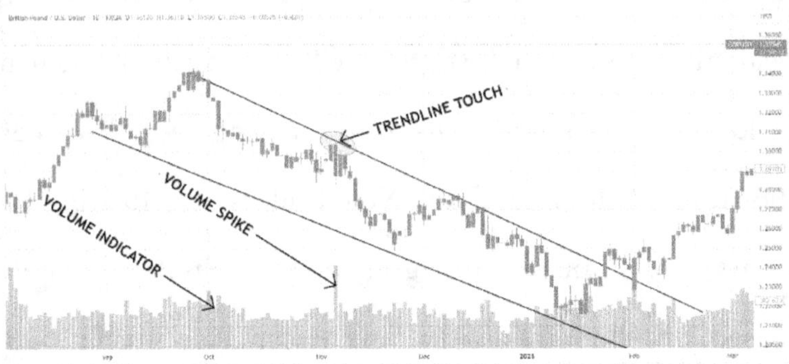

Chart 3: Volume aligns at the touch of the Trendline. giving more indication of a bearish market

Support Becoming Resistance Dynamics

One of the most profitable concepts in trend line trading is the role reversal that occurs when support becomes resistance or vice versa. When an ascending trend line finally breaks to the downside, that same line often acts as resistance on any subsequent rally attempts. This happens because traders who were long from the previous bounces now view any return to that level as an opportunity to exit their losing positions at breakeven.

The psychological impact of these role reversals is enormous. Imagine you bought EUR/USD at a trend line support level expecting another bounce, but instead the line broke and you're now sitting on a 150-pip loss. When price rallies back to that same trend line weeks later, you're not thinking about buying again - you're thinking about getting out of your underwater position. Multiply this scenario by thousands of traders and you understand why broken support becomes formidable resistance.

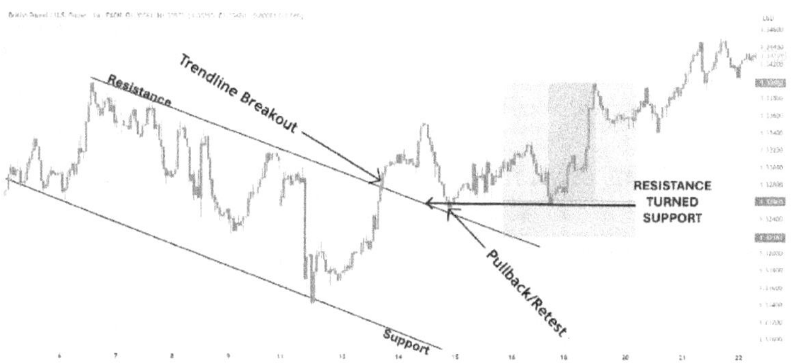

Chart 4: GBP/USD daily chart displaying clear support and resistance role reversal pattern.

Chart 4 Reference Point: *The chart shows a descending Trendline that initially acts as resistance through multiple successful bounces, then transforms into support after being broken.*

Multiple Timeframe Confirmation

The strongest support and resistance levels occur when trend lines align across multiple timeframes simultaneously. A trend line that shows up on both the daily and weekly charts carries significantly more weight than one that only appears on shorter timeframes. This multi-timeframe confluence indicates that both short-term and long-term market participants are focused on the same price level.

During my seventh year of trading, I developed a systematic approach to timeframe analysis that dramatically improved my trend line success rate. I start with the weekly chart to identify major structural levels, then move to the daily chart to find intermediate trend lines, and finally use the 4-hour chart to fine-tune my entry timing. This top-down approach ensures that I'm trading in harmony with the broader market structure rather than fighting against it.

Volume Confirmation Techniques

Volume patterns at trend line tests provide crucial confirmation signals that separate high-probability setups from low-probability ones. When price approaches a trend line with increasing volume, it suggests that significant market participants are interested in that level. When volume decreases as price approaches a trend line, it often indicates that the line might not hold on this test.

The most reliable trend line bounces occur when price approaches the line with moderate volume, then explodes higher or lower with dramatically increased volume as the bounce develops. This pattern shows you that institutional money was waiting at the trend line level and entered aggressively once price action confirmed the bounce was legitimate.

Chart 5: Volume patterns at trend line tests providing crucial confirmation signals that separate high-probability setups from low- probability setups

Recognizing Weakening Trend Lines

Not all trend lines maintain their effectiveness indefinitely. You need to recognize when a trend line is losing its power before it costs you money. Signs of weakening include price spending more time near the line without decisive bounces, decreased volume at test points, and smaller bounce distances after each successful test.

I've noticed that trend lines typically weaken after five or six successful tests. The market becomes too aware of the level, and large participants start positioning themselves for the eventual break rather than the next bounce. This is why I often reduce my position sizes on the fifth or sixth test of any trend line, even if the technical setup looks perfect.

News Events and Trend Line Interaction

Major news events can either strengthen or destroy trend line effectiveness depending on how they align with existing market structure. When fundamental developments support the direction implied by your trend line, the combination creates explosive moves that can generate exceptional profits. However, when news contradicts your trend line analysis, even the strongest technical levels can be overwhelmed by fundamental pressure.

The key is understanding which news events are likely to impact your specific currency pairs and positioning yourself accordingly. Economic releases that directly affect interest rate expectations tend to have the most dramatic impact on trend line effectiveness, especially for major pairs like EUR/USD and GBP/USD.

CHAPTER 4

Breakout Strategies - When Lines Give Way to Profits

Breakout trading represents the highest-reward opportunities in trend line analysis, but also carries the highest risk of deception. When trend lines that have held for weeks or months finally surrender to market pressure, the resulting moves can generate exceptional profits in compressed timeframes. The challenge lies in separating legitimate breaks from the false signals that trap unprepared traders.

Market Conditions That Create Genuine Breaks

Authentic breakouts develop under specific circumstances that experienced traders learn to recognize before they occur. The most powerful breaks happen when fundamental shifts in market sentiment coincide with technical weakness in established trend lines. Economic data releases, central bank announcements, or geopolitical developments can provide the catalyst needed to overwhelm previously respected technical levels.

Institutional accumulation or distribution patterns often precede major breakouts. Large participants spend weeks building positions near trend line levels, creating the liquidity imbalances needed for explosive moves. You can sometimes detect this institutional activity through unusual volume patterns or subtle changes in price behavior around the trend line. When institutional money decides a trend line will break, they position themselves accordingly and often make their prediction self-fulfilling.

The age and strength of the trend line also affects breakout probability. Lines that have held for three to six months with multiple successful tests become increasingly vulnerable as more traders recognize their significance. Paradoxically, the most watched trend lines often produce the most dramatic breaks because so many participants have similar stop loss levels clustered just beyond the line.

Volume Analysis for Breakout Confirmation

Volume patterns provide the most reliable confirmation of genuine breakout potential versus false break probability. Legitimate breaks almost always occur with volume expansion that exceeds recent averages by significant margins. This increased participation indicates that institutional money is driving the move rather than retail speculation creating temporary price spikes.

I've developed a specific volume criteria system through extensive backtesting of breakout setups. Volume must exceed the 20-period moving average by at least 175% for major currency pairs and 200% for minor pairs. Additionally, the volume spike should occur simultaneously with the price break rather than preceding it by several candles. Pre-breakout volume spikes often indicate distribution or accumulation that might not result in immediate directional movement.

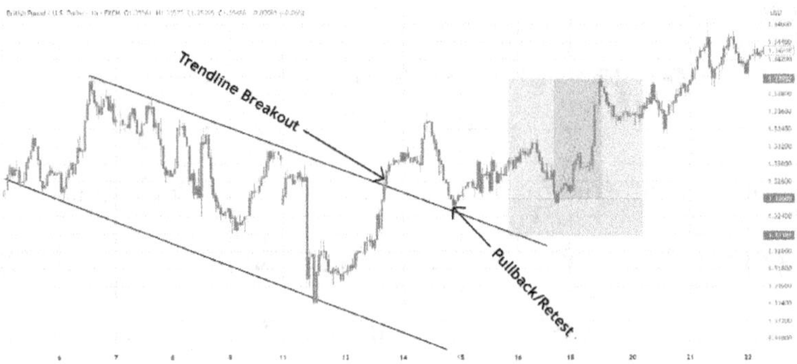

Chart 6: Chart displaying a textbook breakout scenario with comprehensive risk management annotation

Chart 6 Reference Point: *The setup above shows a descending trend line tested four times over a given period, followed by a decisive breakout. Entry trigger,* *initial stop loss, and profit target level clearly marked with exact pip measurements and risk-reward calculations.*

Timing Your Breakout Entries

Entry timing separates successful breakout traders from those who consistently get stopped out by false signals. The most effective approach involves waiting for confirmation rather than attempting to catch the break as it happens. This patience eliminates many whipsaw trades that reverse quickly after triggering stops.

My preferred entry method requires a decisive close beyond the trend line accompanied by strong momentum in the breakout direction. The breakout candle should close in the top 25% of its range for bullish breaks or bottom 25% for bearish breaks. This demonstrates conviction rather than hesitation at the critical moment. Weak breakout candles with small bodies or long opposing shadows often reverse within the next few trading sessions.

Secondary confirmation comes from momentum oscillators breaking their own trend lines simultaneously with price. When both price structure and momentum indicators align in favor of the breakout direction, the probability of sustained movement increases dramatically. This multi-layered confirmation approach filters out many false signals while capturing the majority of genuine trending moves.

Risk Management in Breakout Trading

Effective risk management becomes crucial in breakout trading because false signals can generate rapid losses if not handled properly. Stop loss placement must balance protection from false breaks with enough room for legitimate moves to develop without premature exit.

The optimal stop loss level sits approximately 1.5 times the average true range beyond the original trend line on the opposite side of your entry. This placement accounts for normal market volatility while protecting against genuine reversals. Tighter stops often get triggered by routine pullbacks that don't invalidate the breakout thesis. Wider stops reduce win rate because they allow failing breakouts to inflict unnecessary damage.

Position sizing requires extra consideration for breakout trades because their binary nature - they either work spectacularly or fail quickly - creates different risk profiles than other trading strategies. I typically use smaller position sizes for breakout trades compared to bounce plays, compensating with larger profit targets when the moves develop successfully.

Managing Breakout Trade Development

Once a breakout begins developing in your favor, active trade management becomes essential for maximizing profit potential. The most successful approach involves taking partial profits at predetermined levels while allowing a core position to capture extended moves that sometimes continue for weeks.

Initial profit targets should equal the height of the consolidation pattern that preceded the breakout. This conservative target captures the minimum expected move while preserving capital for the next opportunity. Additional profit targets at 1.5 times and 2 times the pattern height allow you to participate in stronger trending moves that exceed normal expectations.

Trailing stop techniques help you capture extended moves while protecting accumulated profits from sudden reversals. The most effective trailing method maintains your stop at previous swing levels rather than using fixed pip distances that might not align with natural market structure.

CHAPTER 5

Bounce Trading - Profiting from Rejected Moves

Bounce trading from trend lines offers some of the most consistent profit opportunities in forex markets. Unlike breakout trading, which relies on trend lines failing, bounce strategies profit from trend lines doing exactly what they're supposed to do - act as support or resistance. This predictability makes bounce trading an excellent foundation for building steady trading income.

Recognizing High-Probability Bounce Setups

The strongest bounce opportunities develop when multiple factors converge at the same trend line level. You want confluence between your trend line and other technical elements like round numbers, previous support or resistance levels, or Fibonacci retracement zones. This multi-layered support creates situations where institutional money has multiple reasons to defend the same price area.

Market structure plays a crucial role in bounce probability. Trend lines that align with the overall market trend produce more reliable bounces than those fighting against it. An ascending trend line in a bullish market environment has much higher success rates than a descending trend line trying to contain bullish momentum. This doesn't mean counter-trend bounces never work, but they require more stringent criteria and smaller position sizes.

The approach angle also affects bounce reliability. When price approaches a trend line at steep angles with strong momentum, bounces become less likely because the force behind the move might overwhelm the technical level. Shallow approach angles with gradual deceleration as price nears the trend line often produce the most reliable bounces because they show respect for the level before actual contact occurs.

Volume Patterns That Confirm Bounces

Volume behavior around trend line tests provides essential clues about bounce probability. The ideal pattern shows decreasing volume as price approaches the trend line, followed by explosive volume expansion as the bounce develops. This sequence indicates that selling pressure diminished near the support level while buying interest emerged aggressively once price began moving away from the line.

During my ninth year of trading, I discovered that the most reliable bounces occur when volume at the trend line test is 60-80% of the recent average. This moderate volume suggests testing rather than aggressive selling, creating conditions where buyers can step in effectively. Extremely high volume at trend line tests often indicates institutional distribution that might overwhelm the technical support.

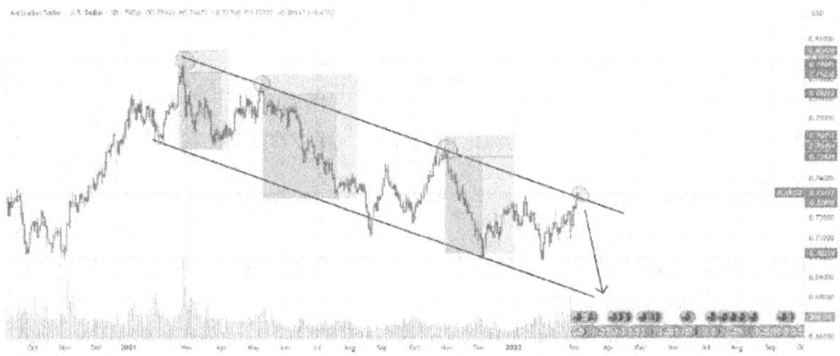

Chart 7: AUD/USD daily chart showcasing multiple successful bounces from a well-established descending trend line over a given period.

Chart 7 Reference Point: *The chart displays four distinct bounce points with varying approach angles and volume patterns. Each bounce shows clear entry signals, risk management levels, and profit potential.*

Candlestick Confirmation Techniques

Candlestick patterns at trend line levels provide powerful confirmation signals for bounce trades. The most reliable patterns are those that show initial rejection followed by commitment in the bounce direction. Hammer candlesticks at ascending trend line support or shooting star patterns at descending trend line resistance create excellent entry opportunities when accompanied by proper volume confirmation.

Doji candles at trend line levels require careful interpretation. They show indecision, which can precede either bounces or breaks depending on subsequent price action. I wait for the candle following a doji to provide directional clarity before entering bounce trades. This patience eliminates many false signals while still capturing the majority of genuine bounce opportunities.

Multiple candlestick patterns often provide stronger signals than single candle formations. A sequence showing initial penetration of the trend line followed by immediate recovery and strong directional movement creates high-confidence bounce setups. These patterns demonstrate that any weakness at the trend line level was quickly absorbed by opposing forces.

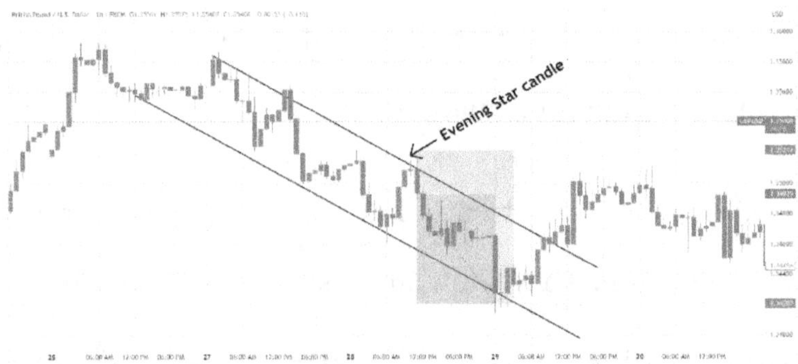

Chart 8: Evening Star pattern at trend line level, providing powerful confirmation signals for bounce trade

Chart 9: Candlestick patterns at trend line level providing powerful confirmation signals for bounce trades

Risk-Reward Optimization

Bounce trading offers excellent risk-reward ratios when executed properly. Your stop loss sits just beyond the trend line, typically 20-25 pips for major pairs, while profit targets can extend to previous swing levels or significant resistance areas. This structure often provides risk-reward ratios of 1:2 or better on quality setups.

The key to maximizing risk-reward ratios lies in patience for optimal entry points. Entering too early - before clear bounce confirmation - often results in wider stops and reduced profit potential. Waiting for decisive bounce signals allows tighter stops and better profit projections because you're entering with momentum rather than hoping for momentum to develop.

Multiple Touch Dynamics

Trend lines become more reliable for bounce trading with each successful test, but this reliability has limits. The first three tests typically produce the strongest bounces as market confidence in the level builds. The fourth and fifth tests often show diminishing bounce strength as the market becomes overly aware of the level.

I've tracked thousands of trend line tests and found that bounce magnitude tends to decrease with each successful test. The first bounce from a newly established trend line might produce 150-200 pips of movement. The fourth or fifth bounce from the same line might only generate 75-100 pips before encountering resistance. This pattern affects both profit target selection and position sizing decisions.

Managing Bounce Trade Execution

Successful bounce trading requires disciplined execution that accounts for the different phases of trend line interaction. The approach phase demands patience as you wait for proper setup development. The contact phase requires quick decision-making as bounce signals either develop or fail to materialize. The development phase needs active management to optimize profit capture.

Entry timing becomes critical because bounce opportunities often develop quickly once they begin. I use limit orders placed 5-10 pips beyond trend line levels to ensure execution when bounces develop rapidly. This approach captures fast-moving bounces while avoiding slippage that can damage risk-reward ratios on smaller timeframe entries.

Exit strategies must account for both profit maximization and capital protection. Taking partial profits at 50% of the expected move while trailing stops on the remaining position allows participation in extended bounces while securing base profits. This approach provides steady returns from routine bounces while capturing exceptional gains when stronger moves develop.

The psychological aspect of bounce trading differs significantly from breakout trading. Bounce traders profit from market stability and predictability rather than explosive change. This mindset requires confidence in technical analysis and patience to wait for high-probability setups rather than forcing trades during quiet periods.

CHAPTER 6

Advanced Trend Line Techniques - Beyond Basic Lines

Advanced trend line techniques separate professional traders from beginners who only understand basic support and resistance concepts. These sophisticated methods allow you to extract maximum value from market structure analysis and identify opportunities that most traders completely miss. Mastering these techniques requires dedication, but the profit potential justifies the effort required.

Channel Trading with Parallel Lines

Channel analysis represents the natural evolution of single trend line trading. When you identify a strong trend line, the logical next step involves drawing a parallel line that captures the opposite extremes of price movement. This creates a trading channel that defines the boundaries of normal price behavior within the existing trend structure.

Effective channel construction requires patience and precision. You cannot force parallel lines onto price action that doesn't naturally fit this pattern. The best channels develop organically when price creates clear, alternating swings that respect both the upper and lower boundaries consistently. These formations often persist for weeks or months, providing multiple trading opportunities within the same structural framework.

The most profitable channel trading occurs when you combine both bounce and breakout strategies within the same formation. Trade bounces off the lower channel line in uptrend channels or bounces off the upper line in downtrend channels. Simultaneously, prepare for breakout opportunities when price finally escapes the channel boundaries with conviction and volume confirmation.

Chart 10: Trade bounces off the lower channel lines in uptrend channel

Internal Trend Line Precision

Internal trend lines offer superior entry and exit timing compared to major structural lines that everyone can see. These micro-trend lines develop within larger price movements and provide precise trigger points for trade execution. Most traders overlook these smaller formations because they focus exclusively on obvious major levels.

During my tenth trading year, I developed a systematic approach to internal trend line identification that significantly improved my entry timing and risk-reward ratios. I identify the major structural trend line first, then look for smaller trend lines within the most recent swing that approaches the major level. These internal lines often provide entry signals 20-30 pips before price reaches the major trend line.

The key advantage of internal trend lines lies in their ability to provide early warning signals about major trend line behavior. When internal trend lines break decisively before price reaches the major level, it often indicates that the major trend line will also break. Conversely, strong bounces from internal trend lines frequently precede successful bounces from major levels.

Fan Line Analysis and Market Psychology

Fan line analysis provides unique insights into changing market dynamics that single trend lines cannot capture. This technique involves drawing multiple trend lines from the same starting point at different angles, creating a fan pattern that shows how market sentiment evolves over time. Each line in the fan represents a different level of support or resistance that becomes relevant as market conditions change.

The psychological basis for fan line effectiveness lies in how traders adjust their expectations as trends develop. Early trend participants draw steep trend lines that reflect initial optimism or pessimism. As the trend matures and becomes more sustainable, traders adjust their trend lines to more realistic angles that better match long-term price development patterns.

Fan line breaks provide excellent trading signals because they indicate fundamental shifts in market psychology. When price breaks through the first fan line, it suggests that the most optimistic or pessimistic projections were unrealistic. Subsequent breaks through additional fan lines confirm that market sentiment is evolving in a specific direction, often leading to sustained trending moves.

Chart 11: Fan line analysis

Speed Line Construction and Application

Speed lines divide the distance between major swing points into thirds, creating intermediate support and resistance levels that price often respects during trend development. This technique helps you identify logical areas for partial profit taking or position additions within larger trending moves.

The mathematical precision of speed lines makes them particularly effective for position management decisions. When price reaches the first speed line (one-third retracement), you might take partial profits or tighten stops. The second speed line (two-thirds retracement) often provides excellent areas for adding to winning positions or preparing for potential trend continuations.

Logarithmic Versus Arithmetic Scaling

Scale selection significantly impacts trend line effectiveness, especially on longer timeframes or during periods of substantial price movement. Arithmetic scaling shows equal price differences as equal distances on your chart. Logarithmic scaling shows equal percentage changes as equal distances, which often provides more accurate trend line analysis for major currency moves.

I use logarithmic scaling for any analysis extending beyond three months or involving price moves exceeding 1000 pips. This scaling method accounts for the mathematical reality that a 100-pip move means more when price is at 1.2000 than when price is at 1.4000. Logarithmic trend lines often provide better long-term trend line accuracy because they reflect the proportional nature of market movements.

Automated Tools Versus Manual Drawing

Technology offers numerous automated trend line tools, but manual drawing often produces superior results because it incorporates human judgment about market context and structure. Automated tools apply rigid mathematical criteria that might miss subtle but important market nuances that experienced traders recognize intuitively.

The optimal approach combines both methods strategically. Use automated tools for initial identification of potential trend lines, then manually adjust these lines based on your understanding of market structure and price action context. This hybrid approach captures the efficiency of technology while maintaining the flexibility and insight that manual analysis provides.

Automated tools excel at scanning multiple timeframes and currency pairs simultaneously, identifying potential setups that you might miss during manual analysis. However, the final decision about which trend lines to trade should always involve manual verification and adjustment based on your experience and market understanding.

CHAPTER 7

Market Precision - Timing Your Entries and Exits

Precise timing transforms good trend line analysis into exceptional trading results. The difference between entering at the optimal moment versus entering too early or too late can mean the difference between a 3:1 risk-reward ratio and a 1:1 ratio. This precision requires understanding how different timeframes interact and developing the patience to wait for perfect execution conditions.

Multi-Timeframe Entry Refinement

Professional traders never rely on single timeframe analysis for entry decisions. The most effective approach involves identifying trend lines on higher timeframes, then using lower timeframes to pinpoint exact entry moments that optimize risk-reward ratios. This top-down analysis ensures you're trading with the larger market structure while achieving surgical precision in your execution.

Start your analysis on the daily chart to identify major trend lines and overall market bias. Once you've found a high-probability setup, drop down to the 4-hour chart to see how price is approaching the trend line level. Finally, use the 1-hour chart to identify the exact moment when bounce or breakout signals develop with proper confirmation.

The interplay between timeframes often reveals opportunities that single-timeframe analysis misses completely. A trend line that appears to be under pressure on the daily chart might show strong support developing on the hourly chart. This divergence provides early warning signals about potential outcomes and allows you to position yourself advantageously before the broader market recognizes the same opportunities.

Volume and Momentum Convergence

The most reliable entry signals occur when price action, volume, and momentum indicators align at trend line levels simultaneously. This confluence creates high-probability setups that justify larger position sizes and more aggressive profit targets because multiple forms of analysis support the same directional bias.

During my eleventh year of active trading, I developed a systematic approach to convergence analysis that dramatically improved my timing accuracy. I wait for price to reach the trend line level, volume to expand beyond the 20-period average, and momentum indicators to show clear directional commitment before entering any position. This triple confirmation eliminates most false signals while capturing the majority of high-quality trending moves.

The Ten-Pip Rule for Major Pairs

Precision in forex trading often comes down to just a few pips difference in entry and exit timing. I use what I call the "ten-pip rule" for major currency pairs - the difference between good timing and perfect timing is usually about 10 pips, but those 10 pips can double your risk-reward ratio on any given trade.

This concept applies to both entries and exits. Entering 10 pips closer to your trend line allows a tighter stop loss while maintaining the same profit target. Exiting 10 pips closer to resistance or support levels often means the difference between capturing the full move versus giving back profits to a reversal you should have anticipated.

The ten-pip rule requires developing an intuitive feel for how price behaves around significant levels. You learn to recognize when price is likely to penetrate slightly beyond a trend line before bouncing versus when it will bounce before reaching the line. This subtle market reading ability develops through screen time and careful observation of price behavior patterns.

Economic Calendar Integration

Market precision demands awareness of scheduled economic events that might impact your trend line analysis. Major news releases can either strengthen or completely overwhelm technical levels, depending on how the fundamental information aligns with your technical bias. The key is positioning yourself to benefit from this integration rather than being surprised by it.

High-impact news releases scheduled near your trend line levels require special consideration. If the news supports your trend line analysis - for example, hawkish central bank comments when you're expecting a bounce from ascending trend line support - you might increase position size or adjust profit targets upward. Conversely, conflicting fundamental developments might warrant smaller positions or tighter stops regardless of how perfect the technical setup appears.

Session-Based Timing Strategies

Different trading sessions create distinct opportunities for trend line precision. The London session often provides the best conditions for breakout trading because European institutional money is most active during these hours. The New York session overlap frequently produces the strongest trending moves when breakouts occur with proper volume confirmation.

Asian session trading requires different precision techniques because lower volatility creates more gradual approaches to trend line levels. This environment often favors bounce trading over breakout strategies because the reduced volatility allows trend lines to hold more consistently. You can often achieve better risk-reward ratios during Asian hours by being more patient with entries and more aggressive with profit targets.

Exit Precision and Profit Maximization

Optimal exit timing requires balancing profit maximization with capital protection. The most effective approach involves scaling out of positions at predetermined levels while maintaining core positions for extended moves. This strategy captures consistent profits while allowing participation in exceptional trends that exceed normal expectations.

I typically exit one-third of any position when it reaches 1.5 times my risk amount, another third at 2.5 times risk, and trail stops on the final third using previous swing levels. This approach provides steady cash flow from routine trend line trades while preserving the ability to capture home-run trades that justify the entire strategy.

Technology and Execution Speed

Modern trading platforms provide tools that can enhance your timing precision, but they cannot replace good judgment and market reading ability. Limit orders allow precise entries at specific levels without requiring constant chart monitoring. Stop orders can trigger entries when breakouts occur with momentum, ensuring you don't miss fast-moving opportunities.

The key is using technology to execute your analysis rather than replace it. Set alerts at key trend line levels so you can focus on other opportunities while waiting for your primary setups to develop. Use platform tools to calculate position sizes and risk-reward ratios automatically, reducing execution errors during high-stress trading moments.

CHAPTER 8

Psychology and Discipline - The Trader Behind the Lines

Trading psychology determines your long-term success more than any technical skill you can develop. You might draw perfect trend lines and identify flawless setups, but without proper mental discipline, these advantages become meaningless. The market has a way of exploiting every psychological weakness, and trend line trading presents unique emotional challenges that require specific mental preparation.

Patience Requirements for Quality Setups

Trend line trading demands extraordinary patience because quality setups develop infrequently compared to other trading strategies. You might wait days or weeks for a perfect trend line bounce or breakout opportunity, and this waiting period tests your discipline more severely than most traders anticipate. The temptation to force trades on marginal setups destroys more trading accounts than poor technical analysis ever could.

I learned this lesson painfully during my sixth trading year when impatience cost me three months of profits in just two weeks. I had identified several excellent trend line setups but grew frustrated waiting for price to reach the optimal entry levels. Instead of maintaining discipline, I started entering trades early, accepting worse risk-reward ratios and lower probability outcomes. Every single early entry failed, teaching me that patience isn't just a virtue in trading - it's a survival requirement.

The psychological pressure intensifies when you're watching a trend line approach in real-time. Your mind starts creating scenarios where you might miss the trade if you don't act immediately. You begin rationalizing why the current price level is "close enough" to your ideal entry point. These mental gymnastics lead to poor decisions that compound over time, gradually eroding your edge through thousands of small compromises.

Dealing with False Breakouts Mentally

False breakouts represent one of the most psychologically damaging events in trend line trading. You've done everything correctly - identified a strong trend line, waited for proper confirmation, entered with appropriate position sizing - yet the market still moves against you. These failures can shake your confidence in technical analysis and tempt you to abandon proven strategies at exactly the wrong moment.

The key to handling false breakouts lies in understanding that they're an inevitable part of trend line trading rather than evidence that your analysis is flawed. Even the best trend line traders experience false breakout rates of 25-30% on their setups. This isn't a bug in the system - it's a feature that makes the profitable trades possible. If trend lines worked 100% of the time, the profit potential would disappear as everyone would trade them successfully.

Maintaining emotional equilibrium after false breakouts requires viewing each trade as part of a larger statistical sample rather than an individual event that defines your ability as a trader. I keep detailed records showing that my trend line strategy produces positive results over 100-trade samples despite regular individual failures. This data provides emotional stability during inevitable losing streaks.

Position Sizing Psychology

Position sizing decisions reveal more about your psychological state than any other aspect of trading. When you're confident and riding a winning streak, the temptation to increase position sizes beyond your normal criteria becomes almost irresistible. Conversely, after a series of losses, you might reduce position sizes so dramatically that even winning trades don't meaningfully impact your account balance.

Optimal position sizing requires divorcing your decisions from recent trading results and focusing solely on the objective probability and risk characteristics of each individual setup. This emotional detachment is easier to discuss than to implement because recent experiences naturally influence your risk appetite whether you consciously recognize it or not.

During my eighth trading year, I developed a systematic position sizing approach that removes emotional decision-making from the process. I calculate position sizes based exclusively on account balance, setup quality rating, and maximum acceptable risk per trade. This mechanical approach prevents both overconfidence and excessive caution from damaging my long-term results.

Record Keeping and Emotional Learning

Detailed trading records serve dual purposes in trend line trading - they provide data for strategy improvement and emotional reference points during difficult periods. Your trading journal becomes a psychological anchor during losing streaks, reminding you that temporary setbacks don't invalidate your overall approach.

Effective record keeping goes beyond simple profit and loss tracking. Document your emotional state when entering each trade, the quality of your patience during setup development, and your reaction to both winning and losing outcomes. These psychological notes often reveal patterns that pure financial data cannot capture.

I review my trading records weekly, focusing on emotional patterns rather than just financial results. This practice helps me identify when psychological factors are beginning to influence my decision-making before they cause significant damage to my trading performance.

Overconfidence After Winning Streaks

Success in trend line trading creates its own psychological hazards. After a series of profitable trades, overconfidence often leads to larger position sizes, acceptance of lower-quality setups, or abandonment of proven risk management rules. This overconfidence bias has destroyed more profitable trading streaks than poor market analysis ever could.

The antidote to overconfidence involves maintaining the same disciplined approach during winning periods that you would use during losing periods. Your recent success doesn't change the fundamental probabilities of trend line trading or eliminate the need for proper risk management.

If anything, winning streaks should increase your vigilance because the market often punishes traders exactly when they feel most invincible.

Stress Management During Live Trading

Real-time trend line trading creates unique stress patterns that require specific management techniques. The gradual approach of price toward your trend line level builds anticipation that can cloud your judgment when critical decisions must be made quickly. This anticipation stress often leads to premature entries or exits that damage otherwise perfect setups.

Developing pre-planned responses to various scenarios reduces stress and improves decision-making during critical moments. Before entering any trend line trade, I already know exactly what I'll do if price penetrates the trend line by various amounts, how I'll react to different volume patterns, and when I'll exit regardless of subsequent price action. This preparation eliminates the need for emotional decision-making during high-stress trading moments.

CHAPTER 9

Risk Management - Protecting Your Capital

Risk management forms the foundation of every successful trend line trading strategy. Perfect technical analysis becomes worthless if poor risk control destroys your trading capital before your edge can manifest over time. The forex market will always present both opportunities and threats - your job is structuring your approach so opportunities compound while threats remain manageable.

Position Sizing for Trend Line Trades

Effective position sizing begins with understanding that trend line trades have different risk characteristics than other trading strategies. Bounce trades typically offer better risk-reward ratios because your stop loss sits close to the trend line while profit targets extend to previous swing levels. Breakout trades require larger stops to account for false break possibilities but often provide greater profit potential when successful.

The optimal position size for any trend line trade should never exceed 2% of your total account balance in potential loss. This conservative approach ensures that even a series of consecutive losses won't damage your capital significantly enough to prevent recovery. Most successful trend line traders use even smaller position sizes - typically 1% to 1.5% - because they understand that preservation of capital matters more than maximizing gains on individual trades.

During my twelfth year of trading, I tracked position sizing impact on overall performance and discovered that reducing my average position size from 3% to 1.5% actually increased my annual returns. The smaller positions allowed me to weather losing streaks without emotional pressure to abandon my strategy, ultimately leading to better decision-making and more consistent execution of high-probability setups.

Stop Loss Placement Strategies

Stop loss placement for trend line trades requires balancing protection from adverse moves with enough room for normal market volatility. The most effective approach places stop based on market structure rather than arbitrary pip distances. Your stop should sit at a level where, if reached, it would invalidate your original trade thesis rather than simply representing a routine fluctuation.

For trend line bounce trades, optimal stop placement typically sits 20-30 pips beyond the trend line for major currency pairs. This distance accounts for normal penetration that often occurs before genuine bounces develop. Breakout trades require wider stops - usually 40-50 pips beyond the breakout point - because false breaks can extend further before reversing.

The key insight about stop loss placement involves understanding that tighter stops don't necessarily reduce risk if they increase your loss frequency. A stop that's too tight might get triggered by normal market noise, forcing you to re-enter at worse prices or miss profitable moves entirely. The goal is finding the optimal balance between capital protection and trade viability.

Risk-Reward Ratio Calculations

Successful trend line trading requires minimum risk-reward ratios of 2:1 on most trades to overcome the inevitable losses that occur even with perfect analysis. This means your average winning trade must be at least twice as large as your average losing trade for the strategy to remain profitable over time. Higher-quality setups should target even better ratios - 3:1 or 4:1 when market conditions support extended moves.

Calculating realistic profit targets involves analyzing previous price behavior around similar trend line levels. If the last three bounces from your trend line produced moves averaging 120 pips, projecting a 150-pip profit target on the current setup is reasonable. Projecting a 300-pip target would be unrealistic and likely result in giving back profits when the normal bounce exhausts itself.

The mathematical reality of risk-reward ratios means you can be wrong on 40% of your trend line trades and still generate substantial profits if your winners significantly outweigh your losers. This statistical edge is what makes trend line trading viable despite the psychological challenges of experiencing regular losses.

Portfolio Correlation Management

Risk management extends beyond individual trades to encompass your entire portfolio of currency positions. Correlation between different currency pairs can dramatically increase your effective risk if multiple positions move against you simultaneously. EUR/USD and GBP/USD often move in similar directions, so holding large positions in both pairs effectively doubles your dollar exposure to dollar strength.

I use correlation analysis to ensure my total portfolio risk never exceeds 6% of my account balance across all open positions. This means if I have a 1.5% position in EUR/USD and a 1.5% position in GBP/USD, I can only add 3% more risk in non-correlated pairs. This approach prevents correlation from amplifying losses during adverse market conditions.

Recovery Strategies After Losing Streaks

Every trend line trader experiences losing streaks that test both financial resources and psychological resilience. The key to surviving these periods involves having predetermined recovery strategies that prevent emotional decision-making from making bad situations worse. Never increase position sizes to "make back" recent losses faster - this approach almost always leads to larger losses and potential account destruction.

The most effective recovery strategy involves maintaining normal position sizes while focusing on only the highest-quality trend line setups until your confidence and account balance recover. This patient approach allows your edge to reassert itself gradually rather than forcing quick fixes that rarely work in real markets.

Capital Preservation Philosophy

The fundamental principle underlying all risk management decisions is that preserved capital creates future opportunities while lost capital eliminates them permanently. Every risk management rule should prioritize keeping your trading capital intact over maximizing short-term profits. This long-term perspective separates professional traders from gamblers who eventually lose everything.

Your primary goal in trend line trading should be surviving long enough for your edge to compound into significant wealth. This requires accepting smaller profits in exchange for lower risk, passing up marginal setups that don't meet your criteria, and always maintaining enough capital to take advantage of exceptional opportunities when they arise.

Maximum risk limits serve as circuit breakers that protect you from catastrophic losses during periods of poor judgment or extremely adverse market conditions. I never risk more than 10% of my account balance in any single month, regardless of how attractive the opportunities appear. This monthly limit has saved my trading career multiple times when my analysis was temporarily out of sync with market reality.

CHAPTER 10

Putting It All Together - Your Complete Trading System

Creating a complete trend line trading system requires integrating all the concepts from previous chapters into a cohesive framework that guides your daily trading decisions. This systematic approach eliminates guesswork and emotional decision-making while ensuring you consistently apply your hard-earned knowledge in profitable ways. Your trading system becomes your roadmap through the complexities of the forex market.

Your Personal Trend Line Checklist

Every successful trend line trader develops a systematic checklist that ensures consistent analysis quality regardless of market conditions or emotional state. This checklist should cover trend line validity, market context, risk management parameters, and execution criteria. Without this systematic approach, you'll inevitably make inconsistent decisions that undermine your long-term profitability.

My personal checklist begins with trend line validation - minimum three touches, proper swing point connections, and appropriate timeframe selection. Next comes market context analysis including overall trend direction, correlation with other technical levels, and upcoming economic events that might impact the setup. Risk management verification ensures position sizing aligns with account balance and setup quality while stop loss placement follows structural guidelines rather than arbitrary pip distances.

The final checklist component involves execution readiness - confirming your trading platform is functioning properly, verifying sufficient account balance for the intended position size, and ensuring you have adequate time to monitor the trade development. This comprehensive preparation prevents technical issues or oversights from interfering with otherwise perfect setups.

Combining Trend Lines with Other Technical Tools

Trend line analysis becomes significantly more powerful when combined with complementary technical tools that provide additional confirmation or timing precision. Moving averages can help identify the overall trend context within which your trend lines operate. Momentum indicators provide early warning signals about potential trend line breaks or bounces. Volume analysis confirms the institutional participation that makes trend line levels meaningful.

The key to successful integration lies in using additional tools to enhance rather than complicate your trend line analysis. Each additional indicator should provide unique information that improves your decision-making rather than simply confirming what your trend line analysis already tells you. Too many indicators create analysis paralysis where contradictory signals prevent decisive action.

During my thirteenth trading year, I settled on a core combination of trend lines, volume analysis, and one momentum indicator that provides all the information I need for profitable trading decisions. This streamlined approach allows quick analysis of multiple currency pairs while maintaining the depth needed for high-probability trade identification.

Daily and Weekly Market Analysis Routine

Consistent market analysis routines ensure you never miss high-quality trend line opportunities while avoiding the burnout that comes from constant chart monitoring. Your routine should balance thoroughness with efficiency, covering all major currency pairs without becoming overwhelming or time-consuming.

My weekly routine begins each Sunday with major timeframe analysis - monthly and weekly charts - to identify significant trend lines and overall market structure. This broader perspective guides my daily analysis and helps me avoid taking trades that fight against major structural levels. Weekly analysis also helps me anticipate potential trend line breaks or significant bounces that might develop during the coming week.

Daily analysis focuses on the 4-hour and daily charts, looking for trend line setups that might develop within the next 24-48 hours. This shorter-term focus allows precise timing while remaining grounded in the larger structural context identified during weekly analysis. I spend approximately 30 minutes each evening reviewing all major pairs and identifying potential opportunities for the following day.

Back testing Your Trend Line Strategies

Systematic back testing provides objective evidence about your trend line strategy's effectiveness while identifying areas for improvement. Proper back testing goes beyond simple win-loss ratios to examine risk-adjusted returns, maximum drawdown periods, and performance across different market conditions. This data-driven approach separates profitable strategies from those that only appear successful due to recent favorable market conditions.

Effective backtesting requires maintaining detailed records of historical setups including entry criteria, market context, and outcome measurement. I maintain a database of over 500 historical trend line trades spanning different market environments, timeframes, and currency pairs. This comprehensive dataset provides statistical confidence in my strategy's long-term viability while highlighting specific conditions that produce the best results.

The back testing process also reveals psychological insights about your trading approach. Patterns in your historical decision-making often become apparent only through systematic analysis of past trades. These insights help you identify recurring mistakes or biases that might not be obvious during live trading when emotions and time pressure influence your perspective.

Adapting to Different Market Conditions

Market conditions change constantly, and your trend line trading approach must adapt to remain effective. Trending markets favor breakout strategies while ranging markets provide better bounce trading opportunities. High-volatility periods require wider stops and smaller position sizes while low-volatility environments allow tighter risk management and potentially larger positions.

The most successful trend line traders develop multiple sub-strategies within their overall approach, allowing them to remain profitable across various market environments. Your core trend line principles remain constant, but your emphasis shifts based on current conditions. During strong trending periods, you might focus 70% of your attention on breakout setups. During consolidation phases, bounce trading might represent 80% of your opportunities.

Building Long-Term Trading Success

Long-term success in trend line trading requires viewing each individual trade as part of a larger statistical sample rather than isolated events that define your ability. This perspective helps maintain emotional stability during inevitable losing streaks while preventing overconfidence during winning periods. Your goal is consistent application of proven principles rather than hitting home runs on individual trades.

Professional trend line trading is a marathon, not a sprint. The traders who succeed over decades are those who protect their capital, maintain their discipline, and continuously refine their approach based on market feedback. They understand that small, consistent edges compound into substantial wealth when applied systematically over long periods.

Your Next Steps Forward

The journey from novice to expert trend line trader requires dedication, patience, and continuous learning. Start by implementing the basic concepts from earlier chapters with small position sizes while building your pattern recognition skills. Gradually incorporate more advanced techniques as your confidence and competence develop through actual market experience.

Your trend line trading education never truly ends because markets evolve and new opportunities constantly emerge. Stay curious, keep detailed records, and never stop questioning whether your current approach represents the best way to implement these timeless principles. The market will teach you lessons that no book can provide, but the foundation you've built through this comprehensive study will serve you throughout your entire trading career.

Exclusive Video Access Page

Thank you for buying my book! As a token of thanks, I've curated a collection of special video content just for you.

To get your free videos, just click the link below:

[Access Your Videos Here]

https://drive.google.com/drive/folders/1yg_Rox6b6ynEut-9hXtAZ8BaAObiWCdh?usp=drive_link

I sincerely appreciate your support, and I hope these new materials will enhance your reading experience.

Warm regards.

Nathaniel J. brooks

www.ingramcontent.com/pod-product-compliance
Lightning Source LLC
LaVergne TN
LVHW022118200926
848481LV00003B/1192
9798295582684